Rocking Like It's All Intermezzo

# Rocking Like It's All Intermezzo

—— *Twenty-first-Century Psalm Responsorials* ——

Maryanne Hannan

FOREWORD BY
Sofia M. Starnes

RESOURCE *Publications* • Eugene, Oregon

ROCKING LIKE IT'S ALL INTERMEZZO
Twenty-first-Century Psalm Responsorials

Resource Publications
An Imprint of Wipf and Stock Publishers
199 W. 8th Ave., Suite 3
Eugene, OR 97401

www.wipfandstock.com

PAPERBACK ISBN: 978-1-5326-9193-5
HARDCOVER ISBN: 978-1-5326-9194-2
EBOOK ISBN: 978-1-5326-9195-9

Scripture quotations are taken from the King James Bible.

Manufactured in the U.S.A.

# Contents

CONTENTS

# Foreword

*Sofia M. Starnes*

In Maryanne Hannan's poem "Embodied," wrought out of verse 2, Psalm 40, "He brought me up also out of a horrible pit . . . and set my feet upon a rock," we find, encapsulated, the heart of this original and deeply moving collection of poetic responsorials to the Psalmody. The poem is worth quoting in full:

"Inner stitched,
chiseled with longing,

who knows if for heaven, earth,
either or neither,

I stand naked on that rock,
embracing now, denying later

the memory of clay, the muck
I'm made of,

clutching always
after the wind,
after—"

The poet's response to the psalms starts with a recognition of a particular trait which distinguishes humans from all other creatures. That trait is "longing"; for we have been "chiseled with longing," she avers. No other creature aspires beyond itself, experiences lack that exceeds physical lack, reaches forth between hope and despair, qualitatively, to the extent we humans do. But that is not all. There is more to the verse "chiseled with longing," for it refers as well to the one who did the chiseling "with longing," that is, with a lover's desire to be one with the beloved. Thus do we learn in a nutshell, within this wisely succinct couplet, that the entirety of this work is to be a conversation initiated—undoubtedly—by the chiseler, the creator, who is now mostly silent, in order to allow his creature to respond through her own imperfect nature. It is not easy; it can never be easy, when the distance between one and the other is so vast, when only he can bridge it. How to rise out of "the muck / I'm made of," the poet laments in this poem. This lament is a running thread through the book. With or without a given answer, the poet gives credence to her patent aspiration to clutch the wind—wind that is, breath, the *pneuma* of God—seemingly out of reach. Yet, how or why should we think it gone? "After the wind," there is "after—"

*Rocking*—even without the rest of the verse—would itself be a perfect title for this inspired and inspiring collection. It evokes solidity and motion; the hard core, gravel and stone which is our human terrain and the motion of cradle, hither and there, evoking wonder, which can both unnerve and soothe us with possibility. Over and over, in Hannan's work, we find this tension between place and destination, between acceptance and struggle, between knowing and unknowing. It is a push-and-pull whose radix must dig deep into a recognition of our ills, the wrongs we do, the errors we bear. We do not hear enough about this, I'm afraid, in today's soft-pedaling of moral truths; we do not find, as we do in Hannan's poems, a denouncement of sin for what it is: "betrayal of [our] core," "putrefying journey" of those "bruised at birth." The poet even wonders (concerned?) how "sin / [has] become outré." It is all too much for modern sensibilities. Yet, it is only through this honest appraisal of who and where we are, that the poet can emerge as prophet, with courage to "taste my taint." Only then is she able to bring forth credible poems, poems capable of stirring the reader out of a self-aggrandizing stupor, to embark on the difficult but necessary journey demanded by our divine calling.

Most of the poems in the collection are so deeply, radically personal, that one might fail to notice another natural motion occurring throughout the book. That is, a movement toward the communal. Poem after poem reveals the poet's abiding experience of the mystical body, of which she believes we are all a part. This embrace of the other, as part of God's whole, is latent almost everywhere, as in the poem "God's Greatness," which closes with the question, "who else has suffered?" We see it, too, in the ongoing oscillation between "I" ("May I be granted a knower's knowing . . .") and "We" ("And when we have found our enemy, help us in our treading"); between "my" ("this is the chalice of my stuff, filled with how human feels") and "our" (our path is lowly . . ."); between "me" ("Catch me when I fall") and "us" ("Tickle us with triumph.") Even as the poet's cry rises out of a deep personal well, we are reminded over and over that the well is fed by shared springs, that all rivers run into one ocean.

From what I've described thus far, it might appear that Maryanne Hannan's collection unfolds entirely in the dark or penumbral areas of our life, and that these are the prevalent landscapes of our emotions. Many of the psalms do start out as laments, and Hannan's responsorials are no different. But the lament, more often than not, transcends itself, and many of the psalms, as we know, turn into songs of praise and thanksgiving, of trust and even joy. None does so more notably than Psalm 22, Christ's psalm on the cross: "My God, my God, why hast Thou forsaken me," which—though unspoken on that Good Friday—culminates with these verses: "A seed shall serve him; it shall be accounted to the Lord for a generation. They shall come, and shall declare his righteousness unto a people that shall be born, that he hath done this."

*Rocking like it's all intermezzo* follows a similar journey. As we approach the book's closing, we are offered the consolation reserved for those who place their trust in the Lord, having come to him with grief, challenged him with doubt, yet ultimately surrendered to his name. In one poem, the poet, having shed her shackles (and her shyness), unabashedly, in obvious celebration, calls the heavens, the earth, the spirit, creation and the Creator, all Holy. Holy, the Whole. She rejoices in this communion with creation: "For the soul which magnifies the Lord . . . magnifies not itself alone"; her soul "perks up" at the prospect of forgiveness, and ensuing delight. There is an invitation to joy in such lines, as there is in "Interlude," a short poem which I quote in full here:

> "Let all who wonder watch
> my soul's sweet twirl,
> her buzz of gladness,
> how she sheds her shyness
> in the moment's grasp, rides
> high upon a surge of grace.
> Let those who look be glad.
> It is not a mirage."

Indeed, what Maryanne Hannan gives us through her poems is anything but a mirage. It is true light, akin to the light offered by the psalmist over 3000 years ago, which she invites to illumine our unlit caverns; it is true light which the poet encounters in those caverns, between shadows, transcending shadows, destroying shadows. The poems speak of a brave awakening, of a journey spent carrying hunger and hope toward the Lord, as only a creature "chiseled with longing" might do. So, let us follow this wise and unflinching, prayerful poet, in her journey; let us do so trustingly, for she follows Christ. Let us travel with her, as she insists and proclaims that the journey will be worth it, that the longing we bear, a longing that defines us, will be ultimately sweetened and satisfied in him who alone can "fill us, no chamber absent Your presence" . . .with joy.

Williamsburg, Virginia
2019

# Marvelous

*Marvellous things did he in the sight of their fathers,*
*in the land of Egypt, in the field of Zoan*

—PSALM 78. 12

The story I was about to tell
was wondrous in the best sense,
full of heart-stopping amazement.
But I refused to linger for the climax
and now have only what's been said
before and the itch to tell once again:
how a keyhole floated through my mind
adrift, a keyhole I managed to still
for a bit, and when I looked inside,
rather than the bare-sleeved barrel
I'm accustomed to seeing, out blazed
a mirroring wavefield, figure and light
and—that's when I said *No,*
or at least *Not Yet,*
because I couldn't have.
after all these years of waiting,
could I possibly have said *No*?
The palpitating, palpable scene dissolved,
leaving only one word to bring back.
*Enough,* somewhere *Enough.*

I.

# Understanding

*I am thy servant; give me understanding*

—Psalm 119. 125

I say to You, my God and Savior,
I know Your trick—

this holographic mystery place of ours,
the mind-mauling cloud where I lose my daily way

this devious underpinning of my ever fuzzy
stumble through the universe

never got its own day of creation.
Time—You made it first and mum's the word,

while seven days of creation-dazzle follow easy,
all rabbits in a hat of wild wizard revelry.

# Time

*So teach us to number our days, that we may apply our hearts unto wisdom*

—PSALM 90. 12

No coincidence

    that we are born

        into piecemeal,

            whacked-out time.


We relish talk of eternity,

    our momentary glimpses

        of the Real,

but nothing suits us

    better than time,

        sliced, slivered

            infinitesimal bites—

nitty gritty bits

    the *what happened.*

# The Created

*It is He that hath made us*

—PSALM 100. 3

Suppose we take this
as a given, Lord:
You made us.

Then we wonder
once made, are we as
dust mites, incandescent,

flaming brief existence,
to be swept away,
when our cycle is suspended?

No, divinity itself we bear
sometimes hidden, smoldering
in service of our spark,

sometimes out there, blazing
in our remarkably
sinewed frame.

# Clearing the Abyss

*Happy shalt thou be*
—PSALM 128. 2

A puffball of a thousand seeds,
the dandelioning ways of unhappy.

No surprise. And yet not eternity's
promise. Now. We'll be happy now.

How much must be undone? How
many of our beloved ways disavowed—

vinegar-doused, decapitated,
weed hound routed? Shred.

Or maybe we follow in flight
as imagined on adolescent nights,

tossing heavy baggage as fancied,
the free fall judged

according to how the drifter,
leaper, diver clears the abyss?

# God's Word

*Thy word have I hid in mine heart, that I might not sin against thee*

—PSALM 119. 11

For Your word, Lord,
is putty in our hands,
so easy to rework.
But in our hearts,
there it morphs
against our grain,
lies hidden from
our will, craftily
whittling away
its original design.

# Sin

*I acknowledge my sin unto thee*

—PSALM 32. 5

When, I wonder, did sin
become outré? It used to flow
through consciousness

as fluidly as Thou Shalt Not Kill
(check!),
Honor Thy Father and Mother
(depends).

I miss sin. There, I've said it.
Not exactly miss it, because
I have it always with me,

as pale as a newborn
blueberry. Bruised at birth,
I will mature, spots of red, vivid

purple. On the best days,
when I don't do the talking,
I can taste my taint.

# Temptations

*Blessed are they that keep his testimonies,*
*and that seek him with the whole heart*

—PSALM 119. 2

Scattered among us—sure,
are those who keep His commands,

show up on Saturday morning
to serve in the soup kitchen,

Sunday morning for liturgy,
blameless and upright for all

to see and admire, so skilled
in matters of self, that they

understand the necessary
stilling, the slow siphoning

of their shadow side.
But even they will admit

that unbeknownst desires
spring up when least expected,

and prompt the heart to snag
bargain basement deals, settle

never-before scores, instruct
the heart to notch near certain

wins against that easy-to-
capitulate mind.

# Uncertain

*Ye that love the Lord, hate evil*
—PSALM 97. 10

If from day to day,
you don't know

what you love
or who you hate:

if both wicked and righteous
take turns dancing

their tangled tango
within you, hold on

until Someone comes
to take the hand

of the wicked, raise
it up, saying

*Father, forgive them*

*for they know not*
*what they do.*

# Creating

*The day is thine, the night also is thine*

—PSALM 74. 16

How we like to play around,
the power and glory so nearly
ours. Not always for what can
be wrought, but for the pulse,
the stir, the charge, the move.
*Lux fiat.* How good, to make.
Let us father mother fashion
create, charge with the light
of Your grandeur, our very
own grasped apple.

# Renewal

*And thou renewest the face of the earth*

—PSALM 104. 30

the face that
waste-charred
fault-scarred
weeps;

the face that
darkened
debauched
returns the stare;

the face we
beauty-bargain
ransom-own

that face
we are

# Inclining

*I have inclined mine heart to perform thy statutes alway*

—Psalm 119. 112

How good does it feel
to put one foot in front
of the other?

Depends
on so many things:
the leg attached to the foot,
the gear, the foot itself;
the ground under the foot,
the slope, the terrain;

even the weather that day.
So many imponderables
that never touch
the decision to walk.

# Shadow

*Let me not be ashamed, let not mine enemies
triumph over me*

—PSALM 25. 2

Let our shames be public,
no longer hidden away in creepy
closets of mind and heart. Let our
shames be shadow stripped,
set out for counting. Let us know
our shames as they know us,
and stop their breed. Let us
admit, yes, here we would pantry
feast, here preen ourselves. Let
our enemies do the same.

# Embodied

*He brought me up also out of a horrible pit . . .*
*and set my feet upon a rock*

—Psalm 40. 2

Inner stitched,
chiseled with longing,

who knows if for heaven, earth,
either or neither,

I stand naked on that rock,
embracing now, denying later

the memory of clay, the muck
I'm made of,

clutching always
after the wind,
after—

# Intention

*The Lord fulfill all thy petitions*

—PSALM 20. 5

Ask and you shall receive;
seek and you shall find

in a new land of promise.
No longer beware of

answered prayers,
the inevitable unravelling

of your vast life fabric
by reason of the tainted skein:

hand upon hand, take up
a seamless mantle

spun on the pure rib
of intention.

# Personal

*The Lord Is My Shepherd*

—PSALM 23. 1

If that's true, I'd be the sheep, metaphorically
speaking, wouldn't you say? Some have thought,
and others outright asked—

You're smart, or we thought you were. Why
do you still hold to old ways, error-ridden
certainties, unyielding then and now bogey men?
Why not more noble truths—an eternal way; leave
history behind with all its sordid baggage?—

I can and in moments, I have,
but always I'm back, needing to harangue
a Face, fuss at my lostness, dream I'm being
herded here, hither, and home.

# Pact

*For thou hast delivered my soul from death, mine eyes
from tears, and my feet from falling*

—Psalm 116. 8

What do we owe
these bodies of ours
in the meantime?

We know the betrayal
at their core
as they pretend
ignorance, lolling along
on a putrefying journey
of their own.

But still—
the dearness at their core,
and the sweet way
they fall.

II.

# Hunger

*Open thy mouth wide, and I will fill it*

—PSALM 81. 10

*Don't be afraid of your hunger.*
*I gave it for your fullness;*
*the cravings, the pinched gullet,*
*the corrosive wants, all*
*have come to serve you.*
*Don't be afraid of the pablum,*
*the drivel in your diet, or the sharp*
*cactus burrs when you swallow.*
*Don't be afraid even if you*
*don't know you are hungry.*

# Indulgence

*Who satisfieth thy mouth with good things; so that thy youth is renewed like the eagle's*

—PSALM 103. 5

God knows we try.
Watch us satisfy our mouths
with the savory product
of our labors. Again. Again.
More. Watch accumulate
our burdens, our heavy frame.

How little we
                   soar,
we don't want to admit,
either to ourselves or others.

Forward, upwards, released—

Of what use, our effort,
if not to generate, simulate
the impostrous flight of youth?
And save us somehow,
surprise! mimicking excess
in the hidden heart of joy.

# Longing

*Like a weaned child with its mother, like a weaned child
is my soul within me*

—PSALM 131. 2

Who more forlorn than the weaned child,
her success birthing heartbreak—
when of cheek full of tongue desire,
the sweet drip down her throat,

she is deprived. She should want this?
Her passion for sweet suckle unabated,
roots around, remembers—there's
no weaning from wanting God.

# Flavors

*O taste and see that the Lord is good*

—PSALM 34. 8

Taste and taste and taste.
Relish the way

you eat; are consumed,
a full mouth having room

for more, the alchemy of sweet.
And if by chance, you glimpse

your neighbor's plate, infer
her strange and bitter palate,

don't be alarmed.

The goodness of the Lord
worms flavor at large.

# Geopolitics

*He hath shewed his people the power of his works, that*
*he may give them the heritage of the heathen*

—PSALM 111. 6

Some take solace—
here's a promise with heft—
ply latitudinal
planes of desire
mapped by the divine.

Others flinch,
refuse to throw themselves
at the knees of context,
demand it be otherwise.

The rest of us
nibble politely
our no thank-you bites
at the contorted edges
of dominion.

# Fear of the Lord

*The secret of the Lord is with those who fear Him*

—PSALM 25. 14

If it pleases the Lord
for his people to fear him,

how easy for Him a multitude—

    the haunted, hunted
    white-lipped among us,

cowed by daily anguish
and Awesomeness

ciphered into supplication,
freed from obligations

to a God who loves.

# The Enemy

*For he it is that shall tread down our enemies*

—Psalm 108. 13

On Your behalf, Lord,
we shall identify the enemy.
Sometimes we'll use external

signs, the color of skin,
annual income, place of residence.
Other times we'll probe

interior abominations — maybe
different beliefs, style of prayer
or a worrisome lack of church.

We can also come to understand
who is our enemy by the judgments
You send: famine, pestilence,

earthquake, drought, plagues
of locust, who won
the big football game.

And when we have found our enemy,
help us in our treading  Don't tell us
again to love our neighbor as ourselves.

# Prerequisite

*His breath goeth forth, he returneth to his earth*

—PSALM 146. 4

May I be granted a knower's knowing
Seek nothing where a something was

Might I finally agree to sea deep dive
Trust a depth bereft of breath

Will I someday dare to savor stardust
Taste the ash of another past

No. No ebb and flow. All circuits blocked.
First things first. And that's forgiveness.

# Spiritual Geography

*He leadeth me beside the still waters*

—PSALM 23. 2


Under the pounding anxiety—

admit it—
waits leaden depression

which—don't let on—
          covers rank fear

that masks—ah!
but it takes a long, long time
and perfect conditions to discover—

boredom, disgust with all
but the unidentified lifework,

and under that?

the merest shadow of pride,
          its own final still point.

# You Did

*If I were hungry, I would not tell you*

—PSALM 50. 12

show us the dark side
of Your longing.

You said, *I will hang on a cross.*

*I will not be stopped,*
*seduced by chimerical power,*
*phantom love or riches.*

Heresy or wisdom: to admit

Your sadness, eased by a woman's
perfume, a blind beggar's faith,

to brandish Your own desire,

no trickle, a torrent,
transfigured on a mountain.

# Tears

*They that sow in tears shall reap in joy*

—Psalm 126. 5

If You'd not told us, would
we have seen it for ourselves?
Would we have looked at all

the Pietàs, the Guernicas
and foreseen another end
to grimness? Or would we have

summoned our paltry rage
for more of the same
vindication, revenge?

And even though You have
told us, we must tell You
that we still have our private

moments, when we mistake
our tears for tears of never-
ending sorrow, when we

suspect joy's flighty sister
laughter is a fraud.

# Cycle

*Who smote the firstborn of Egypt, both of man and beast*

—PSALM 135. 8

Was God happy then?

Rather say
He did not delight
to see the mothers
tear their veils,
pummel the earth,

the grandmothers' strangled grief,

the village awash in gore.

Tell us He could see
a man coming
who'd demand the left cheek
be turned to the hammer,

and when this man was His Son,
His own heart would splinter.

# God's Greatness

*Who is so great a God as our God?*

—PSALM 77. 13

Under Whose protection,
no evil will befall us, Who, when
named and proclaimed,
will provide all good things,
protect us from harm.

Excuse me, this is hard.

When our talismanic devotion
fails, inevitable as even the best
devotions, the strongest faith
must, and we're left spinning
around spurious reason and useless
argument, or drenching ourselves
in bitter dregs of affect,

let us notice then—
Who else has suffered?

# Gone

*God is gone up with a shout, the Lord with the sound of a trumpet*

—PSALM 47. 5

Again that God we meet
on the road to Emmaus;
the One Who rode
His blaze of glory
out of here,
while we shouted,
*Stay! Stay with us*
*for we shake with fear*
*and don't know*
*what to do.* But
goneness is God-ness,
goodness
for those who wait.

# What If He Said

*All the paths of the Lord are mercy and truth*

—PSALM 25. 10

*Beware the given path,*
*its cast in stoneness.*
*Watch out for humble*
*beginnings or worse,*
*the worthy end. Progress*
*can mask the face of truth,*
*cast off mercy as redundant.*
*Stay where you are.*
*I'll meet you there.*

III.

# Threshold

*I had rather be a doorkeeper in the house of my God,*
*than to dwell in the tents of wickedness*

—PSALM 84. 10

How long on the threshold,
not knowing the sacred center,
except by promise, uncertain glimpse?

How tiresome living liminal,
Janus-faced, downward
dogged, the mossy peat,

the scent of bodies
haunting on the breeze.

# Praise

*I will sing praises unto my God while I have any being*
—PSALM 146. 2

So please take as praise
my hacksaw rasp, catfish
sizzle. And distant droning.
I mean them as praise.

And please do not assume
my silence is praise-less.
Sister Tongue so often,
her spiel stuff. My being,
praise God, that You know.

# Paths

*Thy way is in the sea, and thy path in the great waters,*
*and thy footsteps are not known*

—PSALM 77. 19

All of which is to say, Lord:
On these great waters of Yours,
how do I not drown?

Say to You, I cede chaos,
bless it in Your name, not mind
the breaking waves?

Say to one God, I surrender
full sway, the pandemonium,
baptism in unfathomed depths?

Wary though: what if while waiting,
dead set against the pathless, I panic?
Those eerie lack of footsteps.

# All-In, God

*From the end of the earth will I cry unto Thee*

—PSALM 61. 2

I swim in whirlpools of wretchedness
for Your sake. I stand on mountain
peaks of elation for Your sake. I am wet

mounted, cultured, Petri-dished for Your
delight. Sliced any way You want me.
I fly in my dreams, come down

in the morning, all for You. This,
I pray, this is how it feels to be mad;
this is how lost feels; unloved;

this is the chalice of my stuff,
filled with how human feels.
Feel it again, this time, with me.

# Footing

*Yea, though I walk through the valley of
the shadow of death*

—PSALM 23. 4


All around us, constant destruction—
daisies, asteroids, our mothers,
our sons, best friends and soul-mate
cats coming to the end of their
mysteriously allotted time.

Fear. No fear. Fear again.
Catch me when I fall
attesting on the way down
that the fantastic may yet prove itself—

and our beloveds lost,
Our Mother World's vanishing
coral reefs, mountaintop decimation,
disappearing rhinos and when you think
about it, even last nights summer breeze,
still share shimmering phantom life,
the All-Along Oneness?

# Boon

*I will sing unto the Lord, because he hath dealt
bountifully with me*

—PSALM 13. 6

Tickle us with triumph.
Bless the seeds we've
sown with run-away
bounty, a cloud-
nine sweep. Wallow
us in laughter, landslide
jubilation. Trick our
eye into dazzle, jazz
our ears' jump for joy.
*Just Cuz*—Sometimes
we need a *Because.*

# Strife

*He shall cover thee with his feathers, and under his wings shalt thou trust*

—PSALM 91. 4

Under what Paracletian wings
do our piteous petitions ricochet,
sheer off vastness? What folds
unfathomed cover dark
writhings, mirthless revelry,
while we wrestle roughshod?
Tender our trust to others?

# Naming

*O God, who is like unto thee!*

—PSALM 71. 19

*Other* is Your Other Name, O Lord.
And when our silver tongue
fresh fills with lightning

names Your Goodness,
Your Justice, Your Mercy,
may we remember

Not That, Not That,
Not Really That.

For our path is lowly,
on the ground,
one foot in front of the other,
toddling rocks and rubble
in our way.

# Desire

*As the hart panteth after the water brooks, so panteth my soul after thee. O God*

—PSALM 42. 1

She is the virgin huntress,
its invincible prey.

She is resounding rock
and driest bed,

a passing cloud, refracted mirage.
She is ever and anon, here and not,

infinite oasis,
thirsting while drinking deep.

# Watch

*My soul waiteth for the Lord more than they that watch
for the morning*

—PSALM 130. 6

My soul is not distracted
by skittish shadows of night.
Nor does she wander,
a nervous daughter,
on door to window's
wishful rumor,
but canny, chooses,
with measured breath,
to linger at the center.

# Silence

*Set a watch, O Lord, before my mouth; keep the door
of my lips*

—PSALM 141. 3

For the mouth
pretending sovereignty,
mastery of its flap,
masquerading
as portal of my soul,
is like any squalid port of entry
where the workmen hang out
for their day wages,
willing their rough sinews
to trade breath
in commercial swap.

# Gaps

*With my mouth will I make known Thy faithfulness
to all generations*

—PSALM 89. 1

When my mouth fails,
or its sister ear closes,
look at my hands—
there I palm destiny,
finger my crookedness. Or
watch my feet. They hobble
direction, sign my life—
where I go, if I leave,
whom I love. Read
the record, and be patient—
until my mouth knows again.

# Concert

*Make a joyful noise unto God, all ye lands*

—PSALM 66. 1

God forbid it's a racket—
grating, discordant, cacophonous
like the noise-makers themselves.

God forbid we invite the tone-deaf
to be part of the choir. Instruct them
to stand steady, look alert. Vetted text,

lip-synced in perfect harmony, we
demand—lest we surprise God with our
mess of difference, its untoward trappings.

God forbid our feisty tongues, unleashed,
run amok, attempt anything
as important as God's joyful noise.

# Harmonics

*For there is not a word in my tongue, but, lo, O Lord,*
*Thou knowest it altogether*

—Psalm 139. 4

Then, Lord, You aren't surprised
how little we speak
with the eloquence of angels,

how rarely our words shimmer.
From near and far,
we gong boom,

cymbal clash, sneak peak
You upclose
our anger and self-pity—

we're glad
You're not stunned
that You sit back to wait

for our sweet arias of love
with that low-down sub-bass drive
*gimme, gimme, gimme.*

# Gifting

*In the day when I cried thou answeredst me, and*
*strengthenedst me with strength in my soul*

—PSALM 138. 3

For truly the world shifts,
rectilinear split, box down
bliss, when the soul,
imprisoned, it had
seemed, in worldly
mesh, hears pierced
its Self's echo, cry
answered.

# Sayeth the Lord

*It is vain for you to rise up early, to sit up late,
to eat the bread of sorrows*

—PSALM 127. 2

Pray, fast, give alms
and know that I am Lord.
Then as dew freshens
the morning light,
you will rise and be glad.

Pray, fast, give alms
and know that I am Lord.
Then as night's
thunder ends its reign,
you can drag yourself forth.

Trust neither star nor storm,
sorrow nor seeming joy
to fathom My ways.
Pray, fast, give alms
and know that you are loved.

IV.

# Power

*Our lips are our own: who is lord over us?*
—Psalm 12. 4

I confronted the wind and urged her to hold
She didn't

I commanded the undertow to cease and desist
It didn't

I picked up a stone and willed it to fly
He didn't

I gathered the councils and decreed there be peace
There wasn't

I spoke to my friend and pledged to be faithful
We'll see

I admired a butterfly alight on the bush, a monarch
It was

# Definitions

*I shall not want*

—PSALM 23. 1

I've carried Your hope always
Never accused, bunch of pretty words—
Chosen these exact ones for weddings,
my parents' funerals. Grasped
after comfort. Tried not to check
Your promise against lancing
aloneness. Refuse always to consider
any guarantee rebuffed. Beginning yet
another decade, I know the best answers
burrow in bloodless definitions—
all depends on what means *want*.

# Numbers

*He telleth the number of the stars; he calleth them all*
*by their names*

—PSALM 147. 4

Not the white dwarf star
does He ignore,
nor the newest nova,
not the beckoning lodestar,
nor the stardust of the stars,
each and every reverberating
full-tone its reckoning.

And to the ones
whose hair he has numbered,
to each of these is granted
at least one moment of frisson,
the cozy innards of vastness.

# Partial

You fill us,
no chamber
absent Your presence,

so what keeps Sister Joy
twiddling her thumbs
on the verandah,

playing trite games
of sticky-fingered
circumstance,

rocking like it's
all intermezzo?

# Answered Prayers

*He healeth the broken in heart, and bindeth up*
*their wounds*

—PSALM 147. 3

So many ways my load is lightened:
a mysterious check in the mail,
crazy fears revealed over-blown,
the unpredicted cease-fire,
a hand held out in friendship.
If I get what I want,
believe my prayer answered,
am I, in fact, Somebody's Darling?

# Protection

*For he shall give his angels charge over thee*

—PSALM 91. 11

Seraphim
Cherubim
Heavenly Choir
Beings of Light
Messengers from God
who stop us
from boarding
the train that crashes?
Who catch us
as we fall off
the ladder
and watch us recover
from impossible
injury?
O guardian angel
of my childhood,
how much better I
slept when I believed.

# Acceptance

*The sorrows of death compassed me*

—PSALM 116. 3

The uninvited guest
in the curtained bedroom,
in the crowded street,

the lying-in one
birthing for nether realms,
the shadowed scourge

of downy cheeks
and planted fields—Come
in. Make yourself a home.

# Wings

*And I said, "Oh that I had wings like a dove!*
*for then would I fly away, and be at rest"*

—Psalm 55. 6

As we fly away,
stay skyward;
don't look back.

Don't notice our children
waiting at the door
for our return.

Ignore our students
preparing their work
for tomorrow,

and the seeds
on our workbench
in need of planting.

Remember to avert
our eyes, grasp
at that rest—

choose to sever
earth-tetheredness.

# Recognition

*There is none upon earth that I desire beside thee*

—PSALM 73. 25

For Who else would my soul
recognize, her head thrown
back in joy, her gaze ever
so slightly averted? Who else
relieve her phantom exile,
the not-quite-right syncopation?
Who else thrill with Thrill,
the sizzle snap of Being?

# Spirit

Under what wings,
what bright, brooding wings,
do we spend ourselves—
paying our dues, burying our dead,
insensible of the gossamer
mesh, the ceaseless caress,
the moues of endearment,
the wind of comfort
in those brushing encounters?

# Royal Garment

*A broken and a contrite heart, O God,*
*thou wilt not despise*

—PSALM 51. 17

See my soul perk up,
seize again her own
lowliness. Drape her
comeliness, now sublime,
in tatters and tears. Drop
the hard shell of vindication
oppressing her, the girding
of worth. What's broken
and contrite, she'll
wear that well.

# Interlude

Let all who wonder watch
my soul's sweet twirl,
her buzz of gladness,
how she sheds her shyness
in the moment's grasp, rides
high upon a surge of grace.
Let those who look be glad.
It is not a mirage.

# Communion

*Let every thing that hath breath praise the Lord*
—PSALM 150. 6

For the soul which magnifies the Lord,
which praises the Lord day and night,

magnifies not itself alone. Somehow

both bird and beast, rock and water,
friend and would-be foe

hear that soul, breathe that praise,

and join with it, in hallowed breath,
some semblance of their own.

# Doxology

*The heavens are thine, the earth also is thine*

—PSALM 89. 11

Holy, the heavens
Holy, the earth
Holy, the spirit
Holy, what breathes
Holy, the daily
Holy abstractions
Holy, each minute
Holy unceasing
Holy creation
Holy Creator
Holy, what's lost
Holy, what's found
Holy, the Whole

# More about Waiting

*Be still, and know that I am God*
—PSALM 46. 10

*Wait in stillness softly.*
*Wait for collapse,*
*a stiller stillness.*

*Wait as the rush*
*of stillness echoes,*
*the pound of breath*

*not yours, the pulse*
*of force beneath*
*your flimsiness.*

*Wait with pure*
*intention, respect*
*for the wait itself, no*

*matter what's felled you*
*into flightlessness.*

# Aligned

*Teach me to do thy will; for thou art my God*

—Psalm 143. 10

I've heard the jackal speak,
her words under the screech
surprisingly matter of fact.
I'm no demon, she says,
or any callow cultural hunch.
I eat, sleep, run and roost
in deserts and woodland marsh.
I nurse my pups and mate for
good, but never call it love.
The stories you've heard
are your stories, not mine.
I've no need for story, no need
for thoughts beyond — what's
mine is mine. An enemy's heart,
fit payment for a nick of my leg,
an ear for an inch of earth.
And before you judge me,
can you hear a *yes* in my hiss
that echoes another last-minute
ditch of parable and precept?
Another dashing, dying *Thy will
be done* omnivorous leap.

# Acknowledgments

Grateful acknowledgment is made to the editors of the journals who first published the following poems. The poems, sometimes in earlier versions, appeared as follows:

*Anglican Theological Review*: "Boon," "Recognition," "Spirit," "Tears"

*ARTS: The Arts in Religious and Theological Studies*: "Renewal"

*The Christian Century:* "Hunger"

*Christianity and Literature*: "Shadow"

*Clare*: "Silence"

*The Cresset*: "Gaps"

*Earth's Blessings: Prayers, Poems & Meditations*, June Cotner, editor, 2016: "Doxology"

*The Other Journal:* "Longing"

*Reflections: Yale Divinity School; a magazine of theological and ethical inquiry*: "The Enemy"

*Seminary Ridge Review*: "Inclining"

*Spiritus*: "Royal Garment"

*The Windhover*: "Concert," "Cycle," "Fear of the Lord," "Definitions," "Interlude," "Pact," "Sin," "Partial," "Wings"

*The World Is Charged: Poetic Engagements with Gerard Manley Hopkins*: "Strife" Clemson University Press, William Wright and Dan Westover, editors, 2016